My Father

Written by Laura Mayer

Illustrated by Janice Fried

SCHOLASTIC INC.

New York   Toronto   London   Auckland   Sydney

For my father,
Jean Mayer
— L.M.

Copyright © 1994 by Scholastic Inc.
All rights reserved. Published by Scholastic Inc.
Printed in the U.S.A.
ISBN 0-590-27539-9

2 3 4 5 6 7 8 9 10   09   00 99 98 97 96 95 94

This is a story about how my father became a United States citizen.

My father was not born in the United States. He was born in Russia, a country far away.

Here is a picture of my father and my grandparents in Russia.

5

When my father came to the
United States, he had to learn
to speak and write English.

This is my father in his
English class.

My father had to study hard
to become a citizen. He
had to take a test about the
history and government of
the United States.

Here is my father studying
for his test.

On the morning of the test,
my father made a big breakfast
for Mom and me.

"Wish me luck," he said when I
left for school. I thought about
him all day long.

These are Dad's special
pancakes.

My father passed the test!
He took an oath and became
a United States citizen.

Now he can vote.

This is my father taking
the oath.

13

Sometimes my father misses Russia, but he is very proud to be a United States citizen.

I'm proud of him, too.

Here we are at the Statue of Liberty.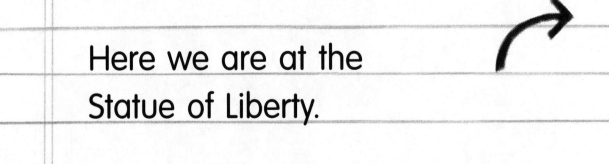